DATE DUE

INVESTIGATING
EARTH'S
WEATHER

EDITED BY MICHAEL ANDERSON

Britannica®
Educational Publishing

IN ASSOCIATION WITH

ROSEN
EDUCATIONAL SERVICES

Published in 2012 by Britannica Educational Publishing
(a trademark of Encyclopædia Britannica, Inc.)
in association with Rosen Educational Services, LLC
29 East 21st Street, New York, NY 10010.

Distributed exclusively by Rosen Educational Services.
For a listing of additional Britannica Educational Publishing titles, call toll free (800) 237-9932.

First Edition

Britannica Educational Publishing
Michael I. Levy: Executive Editor, Encyclopædia Britannica
J.E. Luebering: Director, Core Reference Group, Encyclopædia Britannica
Adam Augustyn: Assistant Manager, Encyclopædia Britannica

Anthony L. Green: Editor, Compton's by Britannica
Michael Anderson: Senior Editor, Compton's by Britannica
Sherman Hollar: Associate Editor, Compton's by Britannica

Marilyn L. Barton: Senior Coordinator, Production Control
Steven Bosco: Director, Editorial Technologies
Lisa S. Braucher: Senior Producer and Data Editor
Yvette Charboneau: Senior Copy Editor
Kathy Nakamura: Manager, Media Acquisition

Rosen Educational Services
Alexandra Hanson-Harding: Editor
Nelson Sá: Art Director
Cindy Reiman: Photography Manager
Matthew Cauli: Designer
Introduction by Alexandra Hanson-Harding

Library of Congress Cataloging-in-Publication Data

Investigating Earth's Weather / Edited by Michael Anderson. — First Edition.
    pages cm. — (Introduction to Earth Science)
"In association with Britannica Educational Publishing, Rosen Educational Services."
Includes bibliographical references and index.
ISBN 978-1-61530-499-8 (library binding)
1. Weather—Juvenile literature. 2. Paleoclimatology—Juvenile literature. I. Anderson, Michael
(Michael J.), 1972–
QC981.3.I58 2012
551.6—dc22
2010048950

Manufactured in the United States of America

On the cover, page 3: This photograph of Hurricane Epsilon in the Atlantic Ocean was taken on Dec.
3, 2005, by a crewmember aboard the International Space Station. These massive, circular storms originate over tropical oceans. *NASA*

Interior background © www.istockphoto.com/MvH

CONTENTS

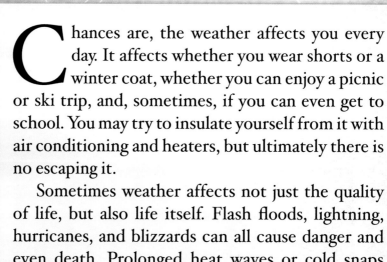

C hances are, the weather affects you every day. It affects whether you wear shorts or a winter coat, whether you can enjoy a picnic or ski trip, and, sometimes, if you can even get to school. You may try to insulate yourself from it with air conditioning and heaters, but ultimately there is no escaping it.

Sometimes weather affects not just the quality of life, but also life itself. Flash floods, lightning, hurricanes, and blizzards can all cause danger and even death. Prolonged heat waves or cold snaps can also be fatal to people—and the crops they rely on. It's no wonder that since ancient times, sailors, farmers, and others have been eager to understand the weather.

Weather is a snapshot of what the atmosphere—the air that surrounds Earth—is doing in a given place at a given time. Look out the window. Is it sunny? Cloudy? Snowing? That's weather. It is short term, as opposed to the long-term atmospheric conditions known as climate.

To understand what weather is, imagine the atmosphere as a vast, invisible ocean, full of currents and swirling eddies. These constant movements of air create the weather. The most important factor driving atmospheric movements is radiation from the Sun. The Sun heats the atmosphere unevenly,

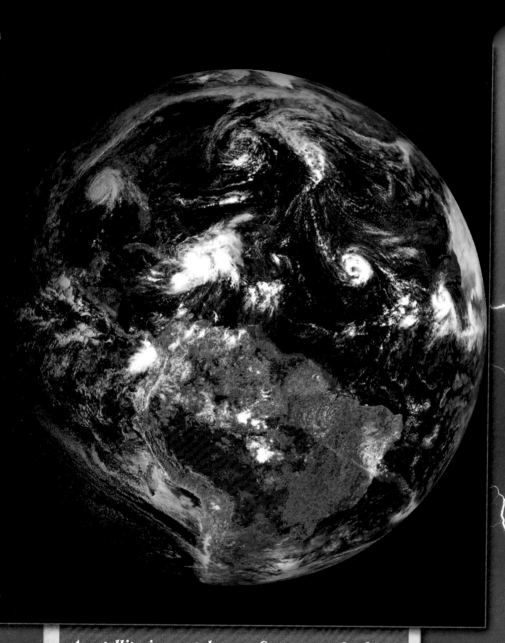

A satellite image taken on Sept. 2, 2008, shows storm systems (left to right) Gustav, Hanna, Ike, and Josephine. **Getty Images**

giving rise to warm and cold air masses with characteristic levels of temperature and moisture. As the air masses move, they influence the weather of the places they pass over. Maritime tropical air masses, for example, form over tropical waters and typically produce heavy rain when they move over land.

At weather fronts—the boundaries between air masses—the air is unstable and storms are common. Severe thunderstorms, ice storms, and tornadoes all typically form where air masses meet. Sometimes the storms are violent. In the flat plains of the Midwest, for instance, there are no mountain ranges to keep air masses from clashing, and in spring and summer these collisions often spawn severe thunderstorms and sometimes dangerous tornadoes. In fact, this region is often called Tornado Alley. In this volume you will learn how these powerful storms develop.

You will also learn how the science of weather prediction has changed over the years. The earliest forecasts were based only on careful observation. The invention of the thermometer and the barometer in the 17th century provided the first accurate measurements of temperature and air pressure. Today scientists have much more sophisticated tools for detecting and forecasting weather patterns. Doppler radar, for instance, can measure wind speeds by observing microwaves reflected off raindrops. And satellites circle Earth gathering images that are fed into powerful computers and turned into maps. Such information is shared by the 180 member nations of the World Meteorological Organization.

And yet, as much as weather forecasting has improved in recent years, it is still difficult to predict daily weather accurately more than about a week in advance. The unpredictability and power of this awesome force of nature shows why weather continues to be as fascinating to modern people as it was to the sailors and farmers of ancient times.

CHAPTER 1

THE NATURE OF WEATHER

The weather concerns everyone and has some effect on nearly every human activity. It occurs within the atmosphere, the mixture of gases that completely envelops Earth. Weather is defined as the momentary, day-to-day state of the atmosphere over any place on Earth's surface. Climate, on the other hand, refers to weather averaged over a long period. The basic atmospheric conditions that make up the weather include precipitation, humidity, temperature, pressure, cloudiness, and wind.

The air is constantly in movement. There also is a continuous exchange of heat and moisture between the atmosphere and Earth's land and sea surfaces. These ever-changing conditions can be scientifically analyzed. The science of observing and predicting the weather is known as meteorology.

THE ATMOSPHERE AND ITS MOVEMENTS

Air is compressed by its own weight, so that about half the bulk of the atmosphere is squeezed into the bottom 3.5 miles (5.6 kilometers). The bottom layer of the atmosphere, the troposphere, is the site of almost all the world's weather. Above its turbulence and storminess is the calmer stratosphere, which has little moisture and few clouds.

Underlying the great variety of atmospheric motions is a pattern of large-scale air movement over Earth. The basic cause of these planetary winds, or general circulation of the atmosphere, is that the sun heats the air over the Equator more than it does the air over the poles. The heated air over the equatorial regions rises and flows generally poleward—in both the Northern and Southern hemispheres. In the polar regions the air cools and sinks, and from time to time it flows back toward the Equator.

HIGH AND LOW PRESSURE BELTS

The upward movement of air results in a belt of low pressure in the tropical regions astride the Equator. On either side—at about 30° N latitude and 30° S latitude—is a belt of high pressure formed as the upper-level flow of air from the Equator sinks to the surface. From each of these subtropical high-pressure

The effect of the Coriolis force

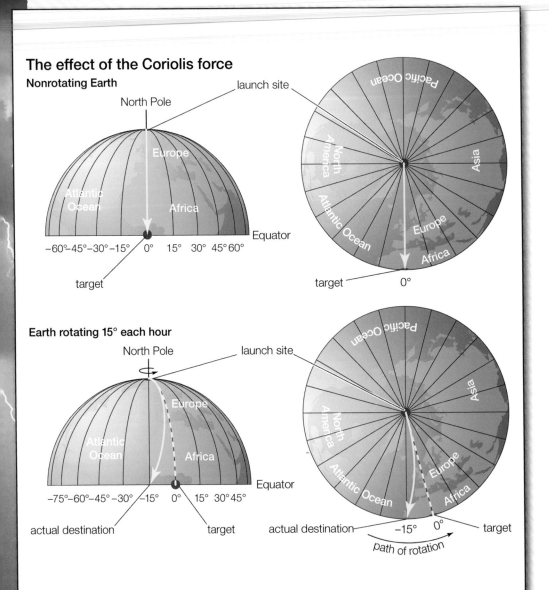

The Coriolis force deflects the path of an object moving from a pole to the Equator. It does the same to winds. © Encyclopædia Britannica, Inc.

belts, surface winds blow outward, toward both the Equator and the poles. The Coriolis force—a result of Earth's rotation—deflects the winds to the right of the winds' direction of motion in the Northern Hemisphere and to the left of their direction in the Southern Hemisphere. This produces a belt of tropical easterly winds (winds blowing from east to west) and two belts of midlatitude westerly winds (blowing from west to east), one in each hemisphere.

Like the tropical easterlies, or trade winds, the surface winds from the poles are also deflected to the west. Where these polar easterlies meet the westerly winds in each hemisphere—at about 60° latitude—a belt of low pressure girdles Earth.

WIND AND PRESSURE PATTERNS

This arrangement of Earth's wind and pressure belts varies somewhat with the time of the year. They shift northward during the Northern Hemisphere's summer and southward during the Southern Hemisphere's summer. Both the continuity of the pressure belts and the prevailing directions of the winds are also modified greatly by the differing rates at which Earth's land and water surfaces exchange heat and moisture with the atmosphere.

Very large-scale and long-lasting changes in wind and pressure patterns also sometimes occur. Most of the time, for example, the eastern Pacific near South America has relatively cool water temperatures and high

In August 2009 a villager collects water to take to crops in a field affected by the lack of rain on in Lamongan, East Java, Indonesia. The area had been without rain for three months as a result of El Niño. **Ulet Ifansasti/Getty Images**

pressure, while the western Pacific near Australia and Indonesia has warmer water and lower pressure. This results in dry conditions in Peru and Chile and wetter weather in Indonesia and eastern Australia. In some years, however, the pattern reverses as part of a phenomenon called El Niño/Southern Oscillation (ENSO), which strongly affects weather in most parts of the world. A buildup of warm water in the eastern Pacific then brings heavy rains to Peru, while Australia experiences drought. The easterly trade winds in the Pacific weaken and may even reverse. The warm ocean water also strengthens winter storms that move onshore in the southwestern United States, causing heavy rain in southern California and much of the southern United States.

CHAPTER 2
AIR MASSES

Air that has acquired a fairly uniform temperature and humidity over a large area of Earth's surface is called an air mass. Air masses are of four main types—Arctic (A) or Antarctic (AA), polar (P), tropical (T), and equatorial (E)—depending on where they originate. They are also of either maritime (m) or continental (c) origin. In general, a maritime air mass is relatively moist and has a moderate temperature. A continental air mass is relatively dry and may have a very hot or very cold temperature, depending on the season.

Every winter, immense, cold continental polar (cP) or continental Arctic (cA) air masses accumulate over northern Canada and Siberia. Temperatures may sink as low as −80 °F (−62 °C). Cold waves occur when a cA air mass sweeps southward in the wake of winter storms. Milder maritime polar (mP) air masses accumulate over the North Pacific and North Atlantic oceans. Maritime tropical (mT) air masses move into the United States from over the Gulf of Mexico, the Caribbean

Oil workers in Alaska's North Slope region walk among mobile units in blustery, snowy conditions. **Emory Kristof/National Geographic Image Collection/Getty Images**

Sea, and the tropical Atlantic Ocean. The moisture in mT air can produce heavy rains.

Other parts of the world are often affected by similar types of air masses, but in different frequencies or combinations, which help determine the particular climates of these regions. For example, Europe is most often affected by mP or mT air masses from the

Atlantic, with occasional invasions of cP air from the east or northeast. Australia is affected mainly by rather mild mP or mT air masses and by hot, dry cT air from its own interior. Australia never feels the effect of true cP or cAA air. After such air leaves its source in Antarctica, it is essentially converted to mP air by its long path over water.

WEATHER FRONTS

Weather fronts are sharp transition zones between different air masses. A cold front, which is the leading edge of a cold air mass, brings a quick drop in temperature and a rapid rise in pressure. It is often accompanied by thunderstorms in summer and snow flurries in winter, and it is often followed by clearing skies within a day or so. An advancing warm air mass tends to override the rear portion of the cold air mass ahead of it. The trailing edge of a retreating cold air mass along the ground is known as a warm front. Thickening and lowering cloud layers precede the arrival of the front, usually with widespread, long-lasting precipitation. After the front passes, conditions become warmer and less cloudy.

A stationary front occurs when the boundary between a cold and a warm air mass

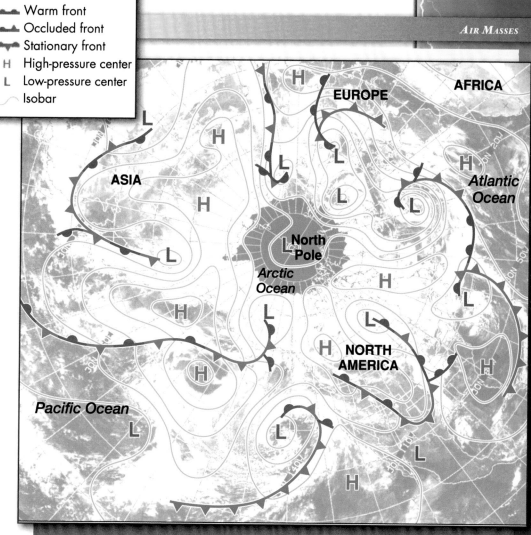

Cold front
Warm front
Occluded front
Stationary front
H High-pressure center
L Low-pressure center
Isobar

EUROPE

AFRICA

ASIA

Atlantic Ocean

North Pole

Arctic Ocean

NORTH AMERICA

Pacific Ocean

Superimposed on a satellite photograph of the North Pole are continental outlines, latitude and longitude lines, sea-level isobars, and surface weather fronts. Over the central United States a cold front leads to an outbreak of polar air, and cloud patterns depict fronts and wave cyclones over the Atlantic Ocean, Europe, and Asia. Two high-pressure centers over the Pacific Ocean are revealed by fairly clear skies. Broad cloud zones lie along fronts extending from Alaska and off eastern Asia. A cloud band spirals out of a storm center in the western Pacific. White areas over Canada are mostly ice or snow on the ground. **Encyclopædia Britannica, Inc.**

does not move appreciably in any direction. Cloudiness and precipitation may then persist for many days, especially on the cold side of the stationary front. An occluded front results when a cold front overtakes a warm front on the ground, lifting the warm air entirely aloft.

CYCLONES

Weather fronts are formed as part of eastward-moving low-pressure centers known as wave cyclones or frontal cyclones. They are a type of cyclone, or a large system of winds that rotate around a low-pressure area, or low. In the Northern Hemisphere the wind

▬▬▬	polar front
▲▲▲	cold front
●●●	warm front
▲●▲	occluded front
⟶	cold air
⟶	cool air
⟶	warm air

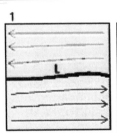   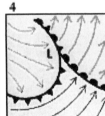

In the early stages of a wave cyclone, an eastward-moving ripple, or horizontal wave, forms at a point of low pressure (L) on the polar front between cold and warm air masses (1). Cold and warm fronts form and pivot around the low (2). Winds spiral into the low (3) as the cold front overtakes the warm front, forming an occluded front (4).

circulation of a cyclone is counterclockwise; in the Southern Hemisphere it is clockwise. Wave cyclones form in the westerly wind belts along the polar fronts that separate polar and tropical air. A wave cyclone develops when a low-pressure area in the upper airflow approaches a stationary front on the ground. This lowers the pressure on the polar front, which then bends to form the typical horizontal wave consisting of a cold front following a warm front. The cold front swings around the equatorial side of the low as it overtakes the slower-moving warm front. As a cold front passes through an area in the Northern Hemisphere the wind generally shifts from the south or southwest to the northwest; in the Southern Hemisphere the wind shifts from the north or northwest to the southwest.

Wave cyclones are associated with stormy weather, which may affect an area of more than a million square miles. They usually reach maximum intensity within two days. Storms in North America and Eurasia are usually steered by the upper airflow northeastward into, respectively, the Icelandic or Aleutian lows, semipermanent features of the low-pressure belt in the high latitudes of the Northern Hemisphere.

Wave cyclones usually occur in groups. As a cyclone matures and moves on, a new one may form along the trailing cold front. When this occurs near an abundant supply of heat and moisture, such as along the Atlantic coast of the United States, the secondary cyclone may exceed the primary one in suddenness, wind velocity, and amount of precipitation.

The Pacific Ocean, the Gulf of Mexico, and the Atlantic Ocean are the main sources of moisture for cyclones in the United States. Lows that enter the United States from these bodies of water, or that form over the western interior, may produce strong winds and heavy precipitation. Such storms occurring with a strong winter high-pressure area may result in a blizzard, with bitter cold and driving snow.

ANTICYCLONES

An anticyclone is the reverse of a cyclone. The winds of an anticyclone spiral outward around a high-pressure area, or high—clockwise in the Northern Hemisphere and counterclockwise

A taxi makes its way through the snow in New York City on Dec. 5, 2002. This blizzard left six people dead in traffic accidents. **Mario Tama/ Getty Images**

in the Southern Hemisphere. Anticyclones are usually associated with dry weather.

In the Northern Hemisphere anticyclones usually originate in high latitudes and take a southeastward course. Extreme winter cold usually occurs in areas of high pressure, most notably in the semipermanent Siberian High. In North America anticyclones have carried subfreezing air as far south as the Gulf of Mexico and into Florida. In summer the slow-moving oceanic anticyclones may influence inland areas in the central and eastern United States, producing cloudless skies, heat waves, and sometimes drought. In autumn, stagnating continental anticyclones may bring spells of summerlike weather (Indian summer). The light winds may lead to an accumulation of pollutants.

CHAPTER 3
WEATHER ELEMENTS

The primary conditions of the atmosphere, or weather elements, are those of wind, temperature, pressure, humidity, clouds, and precipitation.

WIND

Wind is the movement of air parallel to Earth's surface. Were it not for Earth's rotation, winds would generally blow from areas of high pressure toward areas of low pressure, down what is called the pressure gradient— a sort of "slope" from high pressure to low. The Coriolis force, however, causes winds to blow at almost right angles to the prevailing pressure gradient, especially in the upper atmosphere. Low-level winds experience more friction with the surface; this changes the balance of forces and allows a flow at an angle to the pressure gradient. Such winds are called geostrophic winds. In the Northern Hemisphere lower pressure is to their left and higher pressure is to their right. The opposite is true in the Southern

Hemisphere. At around 30,000 feet (9,000 meters) in altitude these westerly winds may exceed 200 miles (320 kilometers) per hour along narrow zones known as jet streams.

JET STREAM

A jet stream is a narrow band of high-speed winds that flow eastward in the middle and upper troposphere or lower stratosphere. Jet streams are characterized by rapid changes in

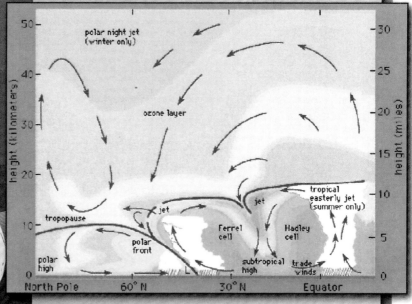

Positions of jet streams in the atmosphere. Arrows indicate directions of typical motions in a north-south plane. © Encyclopædia Britannica, Inc.

wind speed, which are thought to be largely responsible for the air turbulence experienced by aircraft.

First discovered by pilots during World War II, the jet streams have speeds of up to 200 miles per hour (90 meters per second) along hundreds of miles at their centers. However, speeds drop off very sharply away from the center, so that the high speeds are limited to narrow bands at heights between 20,000 and 45,000 feet (6 and 14 kilometers).

Pakistani villagers wade through flood waters near Basira village in Punjab on Aug. 22, 2010. Torrential monsoon rains unleashed by the tropical jet stream caused the worst floods in 80 years, affecting 20 million people. **Pedro Ugarte / AFP/Getty Images**

Jet streams circle Earth in meandering paths, shifting position as well as speed with the seasons. During the winter they are nearer the Equator and their speeds are higher than during the summer. There are often two, sometimes three jet-stream systems in each hemisphere. One is related to the Polar Front, lying in midlatitudes where the weather fronts promote the formation of squalls, storms, and cyclones. The other system, the Subtropical Jet Stream, lies above the subtropical high-pressure belt and is usually associated with fair weather. During summer a third system occurs over Southeast Asia, India, the Arabian Sea, and tropical Africa. This tropical jet stream affects the formation and length of Indian and African summer monsoons.

TEMPERATURE

Temperature changes may also be associated with wind direction. In the Northern Hemisphere winds from the south usually bring rising temperatures, while northerly winds are normally accompanied by falling temperatures. The opposite is true in the Southern Hemisphere. Under cloudless skies temperatures may vary greatly between night and day, while clouds keep temperatures more uniform.

A vendor moves cases of water and soda during a heat advisory on Aug. 5, 2010, in New York City. Temperatures and high humidity combined to make it feel as hot as 100 °F (38 °C) on the streets. Spencer Platt/Getty Images

ATMOSPHERIC PRESSURE

Atmospheric pressure by itself has limited significance in weather forecasting. However, changes in pressure do matter, if a correction is made for normal changes, such as a fall in pressure that usually occurs during the midday hours. Falling pressure generally indicates that a storm is approaching; rising pressure indicates the approach or continuation of fair weather.

HUMIDITY

Humidity is the amount of moisture in the air. Water exists in the air in gaseous form, called water vapor. Warm air can contain more vapor than cold air can. The maximum amount of vapor possible at a specific temperature is known as its saturation value. Relative humidity is the proportion of water

A man walks next to a net used to collect water from fog in Lima, Peru. Such nets can be a valuable source of water in places that experience heavy fog but receive little rain. **Ernesto Benavides/AFP/Getty Images**

vapor actually in the air at a given temperature as compared with the maximum amount possible at that temperature. It may vary from almost none over deserts to as much as 100 percent in thick fog or rain.

Another very useful humidity measurement is dew point—the temperature at which the relative humidity would reach 100 percent, given the current amount of water vapor present. Higher dew points correspond to greater amounts of moisture.

CLOUDS

Clouds often signal an imminent weather change. Rising cloud levels indicate clearing weather, while thickening and lowering clouds signify precipitation. Clouds form when water vapor is cooled below its dew point and condenses into tiny but visible droplets or ice crystals. The cloud base indicates the level at which rising air reaches its dew point. The main cloud types are the high, wispy cirrus, the layered stratus, and the massive, billowy cumulus. The terms *alto*, meaning "high," and *nimbus*, meaning "rain," further describe clouds.

Fog is a cloud whose base is on the ground. Like clouds, it forms when moist air cools below its dew point. Dew is formed when

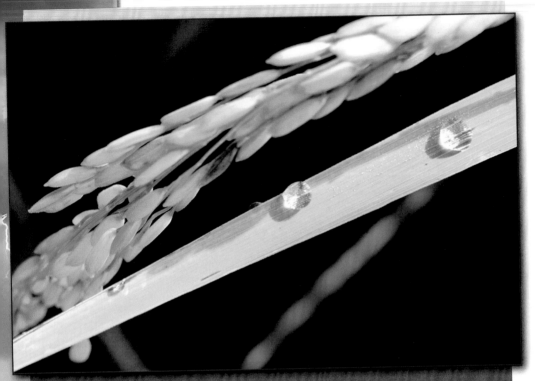

Morning dew gathers on rice leaves at a farm near Manila, Philippines.
Romeo Gacad/AFP/Getty Images

moist air is in contact with a surface such as grass that has been cooled below the air's dew point by nighttime radiation. When the temperature is below freezing, frost forms instead of dew.

CHAPTER 4
PRECIPITATION AND STORMS

The liquid and solid water particles that fall from clouds and reach the ground are known as precipitation. These particles include rain, snow, sleet, and hail. The form that precipitation takes depends on the state of the atmosphere. When the atmosphere is disturbed, storms often develop. A storm is typically characterized by strong winds, heavy rain, snow, sleet, hail, lightning, or a combination of these conditions. Each type of storm follows a particular life cycle and occurs in specific seasons when atmospheric conditions are right for its creation.

RAIN AND SNOW

When warm, moist air cools to its dew point, condensation occurs if there are dust particles or salt crystals to serve as nuclei of condensation. When moist air is lifted by the collision of warm and cold air masses or by movement up a mountain slope, cooling

Rescue workers try to dig out a cab after a hailstorm covered it in a street of Bogota, Colombia, on Nov. 3, 2007. This kind of weather is extremely rare in Colombia. **Mauricio Duenas/AFP/Getty Images**

and condensation may result in precipitation. The tiny water droplets that make up the cloud collide and coalesce into larger droplets. Eventually they may become heavy enough to fall to the ground as raindrops.

If air is lifted above the freezing level aloft, the moisture may form ice crystals. When ice crystals form in a supercooled cloud (a cloud

SNOWFLAKES

Snowflakes are collections of as many as one hundred ice crystals, which appear in an infinite variety of forms and are often beautifully intricate. The size and shape of these crystals depend mainly on the temperature and the amount of water vapor present as they develop. They can form in either of two ways. At temperatures above about –40 °F (–40 °C), water vapor may crystallize around minute nuclei of mineral particles that float in the air; at lower temperatures, water vapor can solidify directly into crystals. The ice generally forms a hexagonal, or six-sided, structure because of the natural arrangement of oxygen and hydrogen atoms in the crystal. If the air is humid, the crystals tend to grow rapidly, develop branches, and clump together to form snowflakes. In colder and drier air, the crystals remain small and compact.

The pattern of a snowflake is captured in a kind of plastic called polyvinyl resin. **Robert F. Sisson/National Geographic Image Collection/ Getty Images**

in a temporary condition of having greater than 100 percent humidity), the water vapor condenses on them, forming snow crystals. As a snow crystal falls into lower, warmer air, it joins with other snow crystals and becomes a snowflake.

A hailstone grows like a raindrop but is then carried by strong updrafts (upward-moving currents) into the higher, subfreezing parts of the cloud—sometimes repeatedly—before falling as solid ice. Sleet (as the term is used in the United States) is frozen rain, having passed through a layer of cold air before reaching the ground. Glaze, or freezing rain, occurs when rain fails to freeze in subfreezing air during its descent but then suddenly freezes on impact with trees, power lines, or the ground, creating a dangerous coating of ice.

THUNDERSTORMS

Thunderstorms are violent, short-lived storms that are accompanied by lightning, a visible discharge of electricity from a cloud, and thunder, the sound produced as lightning rapidly heats the air along its channel, causing this air to expand at supersonic speeds. These storms usually also produce heavy rain and strong, gusty winds. They are almost always associated with very tall, dense rain clouds called cumulonimbus clouds. Thunderstorms are very common in many parts of the world, especially in tropical areas.

Updrafts of warm air set off these storms. An updraft may start over ground that is more intensely heated by the Sun than the land surrounding the area. Bare, rocky, or paved areas, for example, usually have updrafts above them in the daytime. The air in contact with the ground heats up and thus becomes less dense, and therefore more buoyant, than the air surrounding it. This air then rises and carries water vapor to higher altitudes. The air cools as it rises, and the water vapor condenses and starts to drop as rain. As the rain falls, it pulls air along with it and turns part of the draft downward. The draft may turn upward again and send the rain churning around in the cloud. Some of it may freeze to hail. Sooner or later, the water droplets grow heavy enough to resist the updrafts and fall to the ground, pulling air in the form of downdrafts with them. Thunderstorms are composed of one or more of what meteorologists call cells. Each cell has two drafts, one up and one down. In a large cloud, there will be several such cells.

LIGHTNING

A violent thunderstorm, with its loud claps of thunder and bright flashes of lightning, is an awesome thing. Everyone has seen, and probably been frightened by, these sudden jagged streams of electricity. It is estimated that, at any given moment, about 1,800 thunderstorms are occurring around the world. These storms produce 50 to 100 bright strokes of lightning every second.

Most lightning flashes are harmless, but a number of them strike airplanes, buildings, ships, and people. A direct strike to a plane, building, or ship can cause fire or other damage. A direct strike to a person can cause serious injuries or death. Lightning may even strike inside a structure by working its way through the electrical or telephone wiring in a house, or even along metal piping.

(Above left) *Lightning strikes the waters of Victoria Harbor behind the International Finance Centre in Hong Kong, China, on Aug. 28, 2010.* Ed Jones/AFP/Getty Images

Thunderstorms are local disturbances usually covering only a few square miles. The duration of most thunderstorms is short, usually only 30 to 40 minutes, but the conditions that produce one thunderstorm may produce additional ones, so that storms may go on for hours. Also, the strong downdrafts from a dying thunderstorm strike the ground and spread out, pushing the warm, moist surface air aloft, sometimes giving birth to another thunderstorm.

TORNADOES

Tornadoes occur when the conditions that cause thunderstorms are unusually violent. Winds blowing in opposite directions around a strong updraft start a narrow, violent whirl. Centrifugal force effectively throws the air away from the center, leaving a core of very low pressure. This is much like stirring water in a cup, thus forming a vortex-like dip in the surface.

This low-pressure core acts as a partial vacuum, sometimes helping to lift the roofs off houses. Most of the damage, though, results from the force of the wind itself. Around the edges of the whirl, wind speeds may reach 300 miles (480 kilometers) per hour.

The funnel of a tornado touches down May 12, 1997, in Miami, Fla. Five people were injured and approximately 20,000 residents lost power when the storm struck downtown Miami. **Miami Herald/ Getty Images**

At first, the tornado's funnel is whitish-gray because it is composed of minute water droplets formed as the air in the funnel expands and cools. After touching down, the funnel becomes dark because of all of the debris it has picked up. This debris can include soil, tree limbs, and parts of buildings; tornadoes have been known to pick up automobiles, horses, and whole trees. When the edge of the funnel slams into a building, the debris acts as a circular saw, ripping through everything it touches.

A tornado usually moves toward the east (or often northeast in the Northern Hemisphere and southeast in the Southern Hemisphere) at 25 to 40 miles (40 to 65 kilometers) per hour, cutting a narrow swath through everything in its path. Fortunately, most tornadoes are less than half a mile (800 meters) wide; the edge of one may destroy all of the houses on one side of a street while leaving those on the other side completely unscathed. A tornado passing over water is called a waterspout.

HURRICANES AND TYPHOONS

Tropical cyclones are powerful storms that form exclusively over tropical oceans, usually between 10 and 25 degrees from the Equator. They are best known by such names as hurricanes, typhoons, tropical storms, or simply cyclones, depending on location. They are most likely to form in late summer and early fall, when ocean temperatures exceed 80 °F (27 °C). They also form best when there is little wind shear, or change in wind with height.

Tropical cyclones may develop tremendous strength and become the most destructive of all storms. Viewed from above, a tropical cyclone looks like a huge doughnut because of the relatively quiet, sometimes cloudless center known as the eye. While the

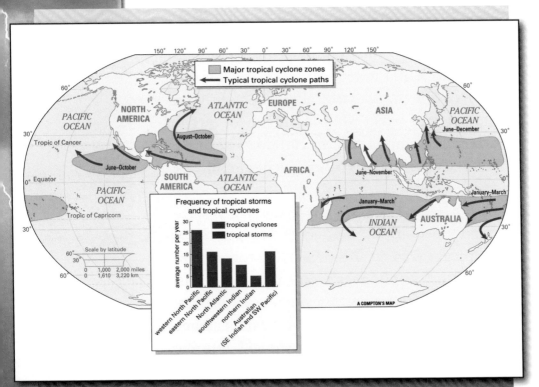

Major tracks and frequency of tropical cyclones (hurricanes and typhoons) and tropical storms. **Encyclopædia Britannica, Inc.**

storm itself may be 60 to more than 1,200 miles (100 to 2,000 kilometers) in diameter, the eye is usually 10 to 62 miles (16 to 100 kilometers) across and is well defined by a cylindrical wall of clouds. These storms always start over an ocean and usually move across areas of warm water, the source of their energy. They sweep over islands and peninsulas and frequently skirt along coastlines. When they strike a large land area, they quickly weaken; the storms are cut off from their source of energy, and friction caused by the land slows their winds.

In Atlantic waters, if such storms have maximum sustained winds of 74 miles (119 kilometers) or more per hour, they are called hurricanes. In the western Pacific they are called typhoons. Other names for these storms include *baquios* in the Philippines and cyclones in India. If the winds are weaker, they are called tropical storms, or just tropical depressions for even weaker systems. Typhoons in the western Pacific are generally stronger than their Atlantic hurricane counterparts. This is because the Pacific Ocean is much larger than the Atlantic, and the typhoons have more time to develop before striking land.

TROPICAL CYCLONE WATCH
FROM THE PAGASA WEATHER AND FLOOD FORECASTING CENTER
Saturday, November 24, 2007

TYPHOON
"MINA"
{MITAG}

AS OF
11:00 AM TODAY

MAX. WINDS: 175 KPH

GUSTINESS: UP TO 210 KPH

LOCATION : 190 KMS EAST NORTHEAST OF VIRAC, CATANDUANES (14.4°N 126.2°E)

MOVEMENT NORTH WEST AT 11 KPH

TY "LANDO"

Typhoon "MINA"

A weather bureau employee checks the pattern of tropical storm Mitag on a statistical map displayed at the Philippine Atmospheric, Geophysical and Astronomical Services Administration (PAGASA) office in Manila, on Nov. 24, 2007. AFP/Getty Images

Tropical cyclones are characterized by very strong winds and torrential rains; severe thunderstorms and waterspouts are embedded in the storm's cloud system. After a tropical cyclone roars ashore, it looks as though the storm has ended when the eye passes overhead. The heavy rains and wind are suddenly followed by some clearing of the sky and an almost eerie calm. Within an hour or two, however, the eye passes and the opposite side of the storm hits, bringing destructive winds and flooding rains again.

CHAPTER 5

MEASURING AND COLLECTING WEATHER DATA

Meteorologists depend on a variety of tools to gather information about weather. Weather instruments measure such elements as precipitation, temperature, pressure, changes in pressure, wind direction and speed, humidity, dew point, and cloud type.

Weather stations in the United States transmit coded weather data every hour for aviation use, every six hours for general forecasting, and daily for climatological records. Many of these stations are automated. In addition, volunteer observers at thousands of substations take daily measurements of temperature extremes and precipitation. Other weather networks are operated for warning of specific weather emergencies and for furthering agricultural programs.

WEATHER INSTRUMENTS

Among the instruments used to gather weather data is the anemometer, which measures

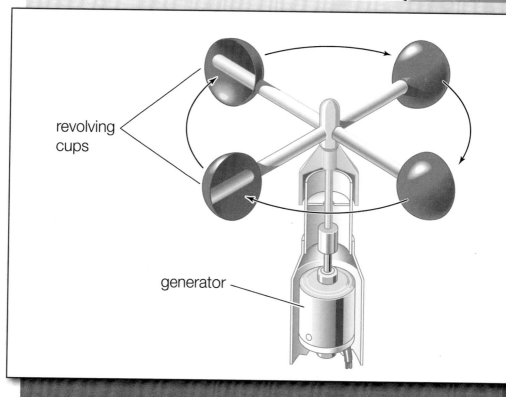

revolving
cups

generator

The revolving-cup electric anemometer is used to measure wind speeds. The revolving cups drive an electric generator that operates an electric meter. **Encyclopædia Britannica, Inc.**

surface wind speeds. An anemometer consists of three or four wind-driven cups mounted on a vertical axis whose rate of rotation varies with wind speed. Wind direction is indicated by a vane, a pointer that swings with the wind and is mounted on a vertical axis attached to a compass rose. Newer devices with no moving parts use pulses of sound to determine both wind speed and direction.

Atmospheric pressure is measured by an aneroid barometer, a flexible metal vacuum box that expands or contracts with changes in pressure. Atmospheric pressure can also be measured by a mercury barometer, a glass tube in which the height of a column of mercury varies with pressure.

Temperature is measured by a thermometer. In the past, the most common type was a glass tube in which the height of a column of mercury or alcohol varies with changes in temperature.

Various types of electronic thermometers (thermistors and thermocouples) are now often used instead. Even then, the liquid-in-glass type is valuable for calibration and backup.

Humidity data, including relative humidity, vapor pressure, and dew point, is secured with the use of various types of instruments, generally known as hygrometers. A commonly used type at government reporting sites is the dew-point hygrometer, in which a polished metal surface is cooled until condensation begins to collect on its surface; its temperature then indicates the dew point directly. Another accurate type is the psychrometer, consisting of two similar thermometers. The bulb of one thermometer is kept wet, and the other dry. The differences between the temperatures they record are related to the amount of moisture in the air.

The ceiling, or base height of cloud layers, can be measured by an automatic ceilometer. It shines a beam of pulsed light (often a laser) up at the base of clouds, which reflects the light. The ceilometer has a photoelectric telescope to detect this reflection. The ceilometer can measure in the daytime or at night.

The amount of precipitation is usually measured by a rain gauge, an open-mouthed container that catches the rain. A commonly used variation of this is the tipping bucket rain gauge, which automatically empties itself as the rain is measured. Radar is used to measure the intensity of rainfall or snowfall and also to compile this information over time to estimate the total amount in areas with no other data.

Soundings of upper-level pressure, temperature, humidity, and winds are made by radiosondes. A balloon carries a radiosonde aloft to 100,000 feet (30,000 meters) or more. The radiosonde transmits data to

A farmer holds an empty rain gauge on the drought-stunted grass-land where his sheep and cattle should be grazing, in southern New South Wales, Australia, in June 2005. **Bloomberg via Getty Images**

ground recorders. The speed and direction of upper winds are obtained by tracking the radiosonde with a radio direction finder. Upper-wind information is also obtained by tracking an ascending balloon visually with a surveying instrument. Data transmitted from commercial aircraft may be incorporated into the analysis as well.

INVENTION OF THE THERMOMETER

The accurate measurement of temperature developed relatively recently in human history. The invention of the thermometer is generally credited to the Italian mathematician and physicist Galileo Galilei. In his instrument, built in about 1592, the changing temperature of an inverted glass vessel produced an expansion or contraction of the air within it. This in turn changed the level of the liquid with which the vessel's long, openmouthed neck was partially filled. This general principle was perfected in following years by experimenting with liquids such as mercury and by providing a scale to measure the expansion and contraction brought about in such liquids by rising and falling temperatures.

By the early 18th century as many as 35 different temperature scales had been devised. The German physicist Daniel Gabriel Fahrenheit in 1700–30 produced accurate mercury thermometers set to a standard scale that ranged from 32°, the melting point of ice, to 96° for body temperature. The first centigrade scale (made up of 100 degrees) is attributed to the Swedish astronomer Anders Celsius, who developed it in 1742. Celsius used 0° for the boiling point of water and 100° for the melting point of snow. This was later inverted to put 0° on the cold

end and 100° on the hot end, and in that form it gained widespread use. It was known simply as the centigrade scale until 1948, when the name was changed to the Celsius temperature scale.

A young girl remotely measures the outside temperature in the winter on an indoor and outdoor digital thermometer. © **EB Inc.**

Doppler radar can continuously measure wind speeds by observing microwaves reflected off of particles in the atmosphere, such as raindrops or dust. Doppler profiles record the apparent shift in frequency with respect to the observation point of waves emitted by a moving source, a phenomenon known as the Doppler effect. A related instrument, the radiometric profiler, observes microwaves emitted by oxygen and water vapor in the air. Careful analysis of the data yields profiles of temperature and humidity at different altitudes.

SATELLITES

Since the 1960s weather surveillance satellites have made it possible to detect weather systems from the time they begin. No longer is a destructive storm larger than a tornado likely to strike without warning.

Weather satellites fall into two main classes, based on their location and time to orbit Earth. Polar-orbiting satellites, first launched in 1966, were the first operational satellite system of the United States. These generally orbit at about 520 miles (830 kilometers) above Earth's surface along nearly north-south paths. They circle the globe approximately every one hundred minutes, so that they pass roughly over each point on Earth twice a day (once heading north and once heading south). Geostationary weather satellites (also first launched in 1966) are at a much greater

A computer-generated image shows the first Meteosat Second Generation weather satellite (MSG - 1) in orbit. This European satellite was launched in August 2002. **EUMETSTAT/AFP/Getty Images**

distance, about 22,300 miles (35,900 kilometers), directly above the Equator. These orbit just about once a day and in the direction of Earth's rotation, so that they appear to hover over a fixed point on Earth.

Many countries now operate weather satellites. The United States has two main GOES, or Geostationary Orbiting Environmental Satellites. One is positioned to view the western United States and eastern Pacific Ocean, and the other has good views of the eastern United States and western Atlantic Ocean. These satellites also observe South America. A group of European nations operates the Meteosat geosynchronous satellites. Japan, Russia, China, and India have also operated geostationary satellites. Together, these have provided nearly continuous worldwide coverage.

Polar-orbiting satellites have included a series operated by the National Oceanic and Atmospheric Administration (NOAA), a U.S. government agency, along with a few Russian and Chinese satellites at times. Polar orbiters get a somewhat closer and more detailed view than the distant geostationary ones. They are also the only satellites capable of obtaining a direct view of the poles. A disadvantage is the lack of continuous coverage, as they can observe a given region only twice a day. Some of these satellites also provide other services, such as support for search and rescue operations.

Most of the information gathered by weather satellites consists of measurements of electromagnetic radiation—such as visible light, infrared, and microwaves. Two basic types of instruments are commonly

Sophisticated satellite weather maps, like this one showing 2005's Hurricane Katrina in the Gulf of Mexico, help meteorologists make predictions. Here, staff members of the National Hurricane Center in Miami listen to a 2006 press conference at which maps of the hurricane were shown. **Roberto Schmidt/AFP/Getty Image**

used: imagers and sounders. Imagers aboard polar-orbiting satellites usually use a rotating mirror to direct light from Earth into a detector. As the satellite orbits perpendicular to the mirror's scan direction, the two motions combine to form a pattern that can be assembled into a picture. Imagers on geostationary satellites scan in two dimensions to build up the image. The familiar satellite pictures seen on television weather broadcasts or the Internet are usually infrared or visible images from geostationary satellites. These are often combined in a "loop" to display images created about once an hour in the form of a movie covering several hours or more. The visible images require sunlight, but infrared images use heat emitted by the clouds or surface and show features equally well day and night.

Sounders operate much like imagers, except that resolution (detail) is sacrificed to some extent in favor of simultaneous observation of a large number of different electromagnetic wavelengths, or "channels." These different wavelengths are emitted by different types of gases—such as water vapor, carbon dioxide, and ozone—and their origin is somewhat specific to different levels of the atmosphere, or to clouds, water, or land. Careful analysis of this information yields temperature and humidity profiles of the atmosphere, much like those obtained by weather balloons, but over a much broader area, including remote locations such as the middle of an ocean.

The huge volume of satellite data is handled in the United States by NESDIS (National Environmental Satellite, Data, and Information Service) and in Europe by EUMETSAT, an organization including 30 countries. The data is fed into computer models and has improved the resulting forecast significantly. Satellite data is also used to produce maps of sea surface temperature, snow cover, estimated rainfall, and ozone concentrations.

RADAR

One of the best devices for continuous detection and tracking of hurricanes, thunderstorms, tornadoes, and other severe storms at distances up to 250 miles (400 kilometers) is radar. In the United States NOAA's Storm Prediction Center in Norman, Okla., analyzes such data and issues severe storm watches, which indicate that conditions over a large area are favorable for the development of such storms. Local National Weather Service

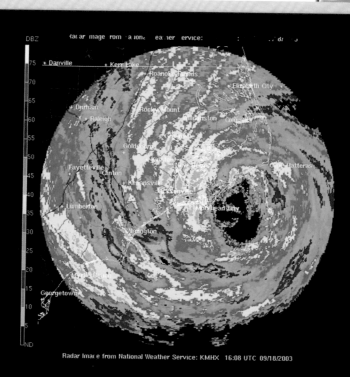

A Doppler radar image of Hurricane Isabel taken Sept. 18, 2003, south of Cape Hatteras, N.C. Getty Images

offices are responsible for more specific warnings, meaning a storm has been sighted or is imminent. The National Weather Service operates the Weather Surveillance Radar–1988 Doppler (WSR-88D, or NEXRAD), which employs more than 150 radar stations to identify low-level wind shears associated with tornadoes.

CHAPTER 6

WEATHER FORECASTING

Through the ages, do-it-yourself weather forecasts were based on local observations made directly by the human senses. Accurate measurements of temperature

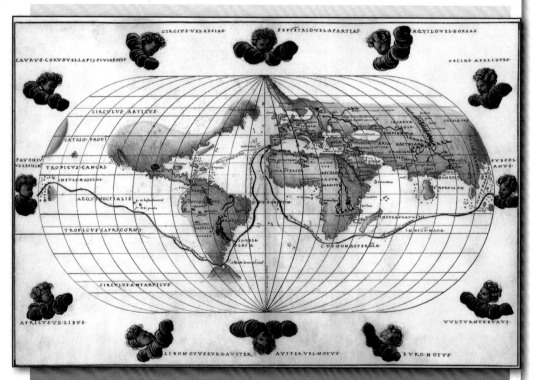

This Italian map of the Winds of the World was created in 1539.
Buyenlarge/Archive Photos/Getty Images

and atmospheric pressure were not available until after the thermometer and the barometer were perfected in the 17th century. Comprehensive weather forecasting did not become practical until the telegraph was invented in the 19th century. This made it possible to collect weather observations quickly and to send them out widely.

The first systematic weather observations in the United States date back to 1738. In 1816 the German scientist Heinrich Brandes drew one of the world's first known weather maps. In 1849 Joseph Henry of the Smithsonian Institution in Washington, D.C., established a telegraphic network of observations for the preparation of daily weather maps.

Government weather forecasts in the United States were first issued in 1870 by the Army. In 1891 the Army's civilian weather activities were transferred to the United States Weather Bureau. In 1970 the Weather Bureau became part of the National Oceanic and Atmospheric Administration (NOAA) and was renamed the National Weather Service.

Civilian weather activities in Canada are directed by the Atmospheric Environment Service, an agency of the Department of the Environment. This agency was first established in 1871 (under another name). Similar government weather services span the globe, from Australia's Bureau of Meteorology to Zimbabwe's Meteorological Services Department. Many of them have Web pages. There are also numerous privately owned weather forecasting companies that in some cases provide specialized services not covered by government agencies.

The World Meteorological Organization (WMO), an agency of the United Nations, dates from 1951. With more than 180 member states, the WMO coordinates the worldwide exchange of weather and climate information. It grew out of the International Meteorological Organization, established in 1873.

METHODS

Measurements collected by weather instruments serve as the basis for weather forecasting. Meteorologists use a number of methods to process and analyze past and current weather data and thereby predict future weather conditions.

SYNOPTIC FORECASTING

One of the most common methods of weather forecasting is synoptic forecasting. It is based on a summary, or synopsis, of the total weather picture at a given time. The development and movement of weather systems is shown on a sequence of synoptic charts, or weather maps. These weather systems are then projected into the future. The weather observations used for the charts are made at thousands of weather stations around the world four times a day—at midnight, 6 AM, noon, and 6 PM, Greenwich mean time (GMT). The most common synoptic chart is the surface weather map. Various upper levels of the atmosphere also are charted.

Sailors, such as these two racers, rely on detailed weather charts to take advantage of the winds. Australia's Glenn Ashby (front) and Darren Bundock won a silver medal in a race in 2007 in Qingdao, Shandong, China. Frederic J. Brown/AFP/Getty Images

STATISTICAL AND NUMERICAL FORECASTING

Another method, statistical forecasting, employs mathematical equations based on the past behavior of the atmosphere. Still another, numerical forecasting, uses mathematical models based on the physical laws that describe atmospheric behavior. For forecasts of up to about 10 days, numerical methods are most often used; for somewhat longer periods, statistical methods are more accurate. Beyond about 90 days, weather events can be predicted almost as well through climatological forecasting, using the averages of past weather records.

WEATHER MAPS

Until the 1960s weather maps were plotted by hand and analyzed at local weather offices. The future locations of storms, fronts, and other weather phenomena were calculated by manually projecting the movements of weather systems from successive maps. Computer-drawn maps now predict wind, temperature, and humidity patterns for many atmospheric levels. Statistical methods are then used to map probable maximum and minimum temperatures, precipitation, winds, and other weather elements.

In weather analyses, lines connecting points of equal atmospheric pressure, called isobars, are drawn on a map. Lines on the map may also connect points of equal value for other factors, such as humidity, temperature, or amount of rainfall. Maps for values both at the surface of Earth and at many higher levels of the atmosphere are examined. Analysis is largely done automatically on computers as part of numerical prediction. The computer-drawn maps, along with many other graphical and text products, are distributed electronically to public and private weather forecasting centers. Much of the information is also provided to various universities, which often publish the data—along with further analysis—on the Internet.

COMPUTER MODELS

Numerical weather prediction is essentially a problem in fluid dynamics. Complete and precise data on the initial state of Earth's atmosphere, water bodies, and land surfaces, plus a complete understanding of the physical laws describing the transfer of heat and moisture, theoretically could yield near-perfect numerical weather forecasts. Such information, however, is not fully available.

Numerical weather prediction was not practical at all before high-speed computers were developed in the late 1940s. Six basic equations—expressing the three dimensions of motion and the conservation of heat, moisture, and mass—are used in numerical mathematical models. Computers solve these equations to obtain instantaneous changes at thousands of regularly spaced grid points and at dozens of levels of the atmosphere. The changes are repeatedly computed for successive short time intervals for the desired time range of the forecast. This marching forward in time is the essence of numerical prediction.

In the United States the NCEP regularly runs at least three different major computer models, from one to four times per day, forecasting for periods from two days to two weeks. Some of these cover North America only, but others forecast for the entire planet. Other countries have similar computer models. A particularly notable example is the model run by the European Centre for Medium-Range Weather Forecasts (ECMWF), a collaboration of more than 25 countries.

Forecasters study the output from the various models, using experience and skill to decide which might be more reliable in a given weather situation. Final forecast decisions are usually human ones, but they are heavily based on the computers' output.

LONG-RANGE WEATHER FORECASTING

Numerical weather prediction, such as atmospheric modeling on computers, is one of the most accurate methods of weather forecasting. But no matter what method is used, day-to-day forecasting decreases in reliability as the time range increases. The increase in

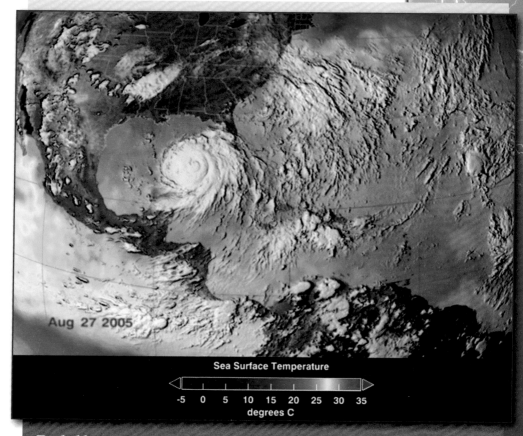

Sea Surface Temperature

-5　0　5　10　15　20　25　30　35
degrees C

Fueled by warm sea temperatures, Hurricane Katrina strengthened as it crossed into the Gulf of Mexico. This image depicts the average sea surface temperatures for Aug. 25–27, 2005. Areas in yellow, orange, and red represent surface temperatures of at least 82 °F (27.8 °C)—temperatures at which hurricanes (tropical cyclones) can intensify. The temperatures were measured by the Advanced Microwave Scanning Radiometer instrument on NASA's Aqua satellite. NASA/SVS forecast errors over time is due to the unreliability of measurements of initial atmospheric conditions over many areas, the wide spacing of data points, and an insufficient understanding of why the atmosphere acts as it does. Such errors can cause errors in computer-calculated forecasts. They grow larger as the computations move forward in time until the numerical forecasts become useless. Persistent or systematic errors are reduced by manual corrections. A typical error of atmospheric models is that the weather systems usually move faster than predicted.

CHALLENGES

In providing public forecasts, weather forecasters take into account this increasing uncertainty with time. The range of predicted temperatures, for example, is increased as the time range increases, and precipitation is usually forecast as a probability percentage.

Continuous weather elements such as temperature can be forecast with greater accuracy than discontinuous ones such as precipitation. Forecasts for the higher levels of the atmosphere, with their smoother patterns, are more accurate than for the surface zones. Beyond about a week, daily weather cannot be accurately predicted, though average weather departures from normal can be predicted to some extent. Long-range forecasts deal with the total effects of weather systems not yet born, unlike forecasts for up to about a week. But useful inferences can still be made about the future evolution of atmospheric circulations.

TRACKING ATMOSPHERIC PATTERNS

The averaging of successive daily flow patterns in the atmosphere smooths and filters out temporary disturbances, revealing broad westerly wind currents that meander between high and low latitudes. At any one time these currents form three to five large waves around each hemisphere. They move slowly and sometimes remain stationary for long periods, steering lows and highs along preferred tracks. The locations and sizes of these large waves determine the longer-period average weather anomalies such as cold spells, warm spells, and droughts.

In monthly forecasts the future locations of large-scale circulation meanders are estimated by a mixture of different methods. One component is an extended run of a computer model similar to those used for day-to-day weather forecasting. Other methods are largely

An elderly woman scoops unpolished rice grains to dramatize the plight of farmers during a protest in Manila, Philippines, on March 6, 2010. The protesters were demanding more government funds to help farmers cope with the drought caused by El Niño. Jay Directo/AFP/Getty Images

statistical, using known connections between historical temperature and precipitation patterns and conditions such as soil moisture and sea surface temperature. Trends over the last 10 or 15 years are also considered.

CLIMATE PREDICTION CENTER

In the United States NOAA's Climate Prediction Center produces long-range forecasts for periods of up to about a year. These are not specific to the day but rather consist of maps showing probabilities that temperature and precipitation will be above normal, near normal, or below normal for three-month periods. While the forecasts are of only a

Floodwaters from the Schuylkill River submerge a portion of a road on April 16, 2007, in Philadelphia, Pa. A powerful storm called a nor'easter brought record rainfall and high winds to the Northeast. **Jeff Fusco/Getty Images**

general nature and only modestly accurate (sometimes only a bit better than chance), such information is nonetheless quite valuable for many farming and industry applications. Many private companies claim to produce accurate long-range forecasts. Those claiming long-range day-to-day accuracy or "secret" weather predicting formulas should be viewed with great suspicion. Weather patterns are notoriously chaotic, and even the best science can offer only modest long-range results.

CHAPTER 7

WEATHER MODIFICATION

Weather modification can be considered as falling into two categories: intentional and inadvertent. Intentional weather modification includes practical, small-scale efforts such as frost prevention. Large fans can mix warmer air from above with the cold air near the ground on clear, calm nights, and smoke from smudge pots can help trap heat near the surface. This helps farmers to preserve delicate crops such as oranges from being destroyed by frost.

Icicles cover oranges at an orange grove in January 2003 in Lake Jem, Florida. The sheets of ice keep the plants at a constant 32 °F (0 °C) when the outside air temperature is in the 20s (about –6 °C).
Chris Livingston/Getty Images

CLOUD SEEDING

A major breakthrough in weather modification occurred in 1946, when it was discovered that adding

dry ice pellets or silver iodide to supercooled clouds could produce precipitation. This process is called cloud seeding. The added particles provide nuclei for the condensation or freezing of water vapor in the air. Most seeding is done from aircraft. Other means include artillery shells and ground-based generators. Cloud seeding can be used to increase precipitation, but a more practical use is dissipation of low clouds and fog around airports.

A worker in Beijing, China, prepares a pipe cannon to be fired into the sky in an attempt to scatter rain clouds. Rockets and cannons can be used either to seed clouds in an effort to produce precipitation or to scatter clouds and prevent precipitation. China Photos/Getty Images

Initial excitement regarding cloud seeding waned somewhat after the 1960s. Suggestions that it could weaken hurricanes or significantly increase precipitation in drought areas were undermined by mixed or poor results from experiments along with doubts about some aspects of the theory behind it. Government funding for research in these areas was sharply reduced. Also, legal questions arose. For example, seeding a cloud over the U.S. state of Kansas that was headed for the state of Missouri might rob people in Missouri of rain they might have otherwise received. For these reasons, use of cloud seeding remains rather limited.

GLOBAL WARMING

Inadvertent weather modification has also stirred a great deal of interest. This involves changes in weather and climate that are brought about by changes in land use and the release of gases and particles into the atmosphere. The building or expansion of cities and the conversion of farmland for industrial use can cause changes in weather, especially by raising nighttime temperatures. Cities may also alter local wind and precipitation patterns somewhat.

Of greater significance is the issue of global warming, caused primarily by release

of carbon dioxide from the burning of fossil fuels such as coal and oil, along with smaller effects from the release of other gases, such as methane from rice paddies or livestock. These gases are transparent to visible light and therefore let sunshine through to heat the ground. However, the ground radiates the stored heat in the infrared wavelengths, to which the gases are largely opaque. The gases are warmed by this radiation and in turn radiate infrared waves back toward the ground, effectively trapping a portion of the energy. This phenomenon is commonly called the greenhouse effect.

The most important greenhouse gas is water vapor. Along with naturally occurring concentrations of the other greenhouse gases (such as carbon dioxide), water vapor keeps Earth's average temperature about 60 °F (33 °C) warmer than it would otherwise be. The problem, according to the great majority of the world's weather scientists, is that increasing concentrations of other greenhouse gases is likely to make Earth warmer than it has been since the beginning of civilization, causing disruptions such as a rise in sea level and ecological changes. A report published by the Intergovernmental Panel on Climate Change (IPCC) in 2007 predicted an increase of 3.2° to 7.2 °F (1.8° to 4.0 °C) in the global average surface temperature by 2100 if greenhouse-gas emissions are not greatly reduced.

According to surface temperature records kept by NASA's Goddard Institute for Space Studies (GISS), in the past three decades, temperatures have shown an upward trend of about 0.36 °F (0.2 °C) per decade. In total, average global temperatures have increased by about 1.5 °F (0.8 °C) since 1880. Not only was 2009 the second warmest year on record, but January 2000 to December 2009 was the warmest decade on record.

There is a strong consensus among scientists that the effect of global warming is real and significant. Difficult political decisions lie ahead as society weighs the costs of environmental change against the cost of attempts to arrest global warming, such as through reduction of fossil fuel use.

OZONE DEPLETION

Another issue, commonly confused with global warming, is that of ozone depletion. Ozone is a type of oxygen molecule, but with three atoms instead of the usual two. Near the ground, it is a pollutant that can cause respiratory irritation. High up in the atmosphere, however, it has the very beneficial effect of blocking ultraviolet light from the sun. By the 1970s it became apparent that the helpful ozone concentrations high up in the atmosphere could be reduced by chlorofluorocarbons (CFCs)—gases then commonly used as refrigerants and aerosol propellants in spray cans. In fact, measurable reductions in ozone, especially in the form of a seasonal "hole" over the Antarctic, have been documented. The result is likely increased rates of sunburn and skin cancer in humans, along with damage to plankton in the ocean.

The good news is that substitutes for CFCs have been found for most previous applications. Largely through an international agreement of 1987 known as the Montreal Protocol, release of these gases has been sharply reduced. By

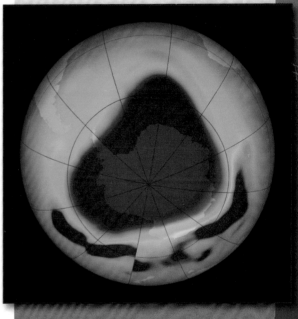

An image based on satellite data shows the "hole" in the ozone layer over the Antarctic in September 2005. Red represents the highest concentrations of ozone within the image, and blue and purple represent the lowest concentrations. **NASA— Goddard Space Flight Center/ Scientific Visualization Studio**

the early 21st century the rate of ozone depletion had slowed markedly, and scientists thought the ozone layer might begin to "heal" considerably within a couple of decades.

OZONE

Ozone is a pale blue gas that is explosive and toxic, even in small amounts. It is usually produced when a charge of electricity, such as lightning, passes through the air. People sometimes notice ozone's unpleasant smell after a thunderstorm or around electrical equipment. The odor of ozone around electrical machines was reported as early as 1785. Scientists determined ozone's chemical makeup in 1872. Because each ozone molecule contains three oxygen atoms, the scientific formula for ozone is O_3.

Ozone is a natural part of Earth's upper atmosphere. This part of the atmosphere, about 6–30 miles (10–50 kilometers) above the surface, is called the ozone layer. The ozone layer absorbs harmful ultraviolet rays from the Sun, which can cause skin cancer, eye diseases, and other health problems in humans if they reach Earth. These rays can also seriously harm other living things.

In addition to its natural occurrence, ozone is manufactured for industrial purposes. It is used in water purification, deodorization, and bleaching.

CONCLUSION

The impact of weather on human life is immense. Extreme heat and humidity cause discomfort and may lead to the spread of disease. Heavy rain can cause flooding, forcing people from their homes. Thunderstorms, tornadoes, hail, and sleet storms may damage or destroy crops, buildings, and vehicles. Storms may even kill or injure people and livestock. At sea and along coastal areas, hurricanes and cyclones can cause great damage to ships, buildings, crops, and roads through torrential rainfall and flooding, winds, and waves. Heavy snowfall and icy conditions can make transportation more difficult and increase the frequency of accidents. The long absence of rainfall, by contrast, can cause droughts and severe dust storms.

Because weather can have such important consequences, meteorologists will continue their efforts to improve their short- and long-range forecasts. Accurate predictions of weather conditions allow people to prepare for an approaching storm or simply to plan their daily activities.

air mass A large body of air extending hundreds or thousands of miles horizontally that keeps a fairly uniform temperature and humidity as it travels.

cell A portion of the atmosphere that behaves as a unit, such as a storm cell.

centrifugal force A force caused by rotation that, in a tornado, throws air outward from the center.

cirrus High, wispy white cloud usually of tiny ice crystals formed at altitudes between about 20,000 and 40,000 feet (6,000 and 12,000 meters).

climate Weather conditions averaged over a long time in one area.

Coriolis force An effect that causes air currents moving on a rotating planet such as Earth to be deflected to either the right in the Northern Hemisphere or to the left in the Southern Hemisphere.

cumulonimbus A type of very tall, dense rain cloud associated with strong thunderstorms.

cumulus A dense, puffy cloud form having a flat base and rounded outlines often piled up like a mountain.

dew point The temperature at which a vapor (as water) begins to condense.

glaze Freezing rain, or the smooth, slippery coating of thin ice it produces.

greenhouse effect The warming of Earth's surface and lower atmosphere due to the presence of certain gases in the air.

greenhouse gases Atmospheric gases, such as carbon dioxide, methane, nitrous oxide, and water vapor, which contribute to the greenhouse effect that is warming the planet.

humidity The degree of wetness in the atmosphere.

Indian summer A period of dry, unseasonably warm weather in late October or November in the central and eastern United States.

meteorology The scientific study of the atmosphere and its phenomena, especially weather and weather forecasting.

monsoon A large-scale wind system that seasonally reverses its direction.

nimbus A rain cloud.

occluded front A weather front formed by a cold front overtaking a warm front and lifting the warm air above Earth's surface.

stationary front The boundary between two air masses neither of which is replacing the other.

supersonic Of, being, or relating to speeds from one to five times the speed of sound in air.

synoptic Relating to or displaying conditions (as of the atmosphere or weather) as they exist simultaneously over a broad area.

vortex A mass of air with a whirling or circular motion that tends to form a vacuum in its center. Vortexes draw in other bodies in a whirlpool-like manner.

Dan's Wild Weather Page
WHNT NEWS 19
200 Holmes Avenue
Huntsville, AL 35801
(256) 535-9330
Web site: http://www.wildwildweather.com
This Web site provides instructional material on weather science, suitable for elementary to high-school students. It contains interactive programs and tutorials on meteorological topics like climate, clouds, temperature, wind, storms and lightning, radar, and weather forecasting.

Environmental Protection Agency (EPA)
Ariel Rios Building
1200 Pennsylvania Avenue NW
Washington, DC 20460
(202) 272-0167
Web site: http://www.epa.gov/naturaldisasters
This Web site promotes preparation for natural disasters and provides environmental project ideas for students.

National Weather Service
1325 East West Highway
Silver Spring, MD 20910
(301) 713-4000
Web site: http://www.weather.gov

This Web site provides active weather alerts, current and long-range forecasts, education, and weather safety tips.

The Weather Channel
300 Interstate North Parkway SE
Atlanta, GA 30339
(770) 226-0000
Web site: http://www.weather.com
Weather forecasts and weather advice can be found here. The weatherchannelkids.com offers games and activities for children.

The Weather Network
2655 Bristol Circle
Oakville, ON L6H 7W1
Canada
(905) 829-1159
Web site: http://www.theweathernetwork.com
The Weather Network provides coverage of Canadian weather, including statistics for specific cities, a seasons calculator, weather cams, and ski reports.

Weatheroffice
Environment Canada
National Inquiry Response Team
77 Westmorland Street, Suite 260
Fredericton, NB E3B 6Z3

Canada
(819) 997-2800
Web site: http://www.weatheroffice.gc.ca
Weatheroffice provides forecasts, historical
weather data, weather tools, and information on air quality, lightning, and other
aspects of meteorology. It also contains
downloadable resources and publications.

Windows to the Universe
National Earth Science Teachers Association
PO Box 3000
Boulder, CO 80307
(720) 328-5350
Web site: http://windows2universe.org/
earth/Atmosphere/weather.html
This site provides easy-to-read articles on
fronts, clouds, tornadoes, hurricanes,
heat waves, and other weather topics.

WEB SITES

Due to the changing nature of Internet links,
Rosen Educational Services has developed an
online list of Web sites related to the subject
of this book. This site is updated regularly.
Please use this link to access the list:

http://www.rosenlinks.com/ies/weat

Ahrens, C.D., and Samson, Perry. *Extreme Weather and Climate* (Brooks/Cole, 2010).

Bliss, Pamela. *Introduction to Weather* (National Geographic, 2004).

Dunlop, Storm. *A Dictionary of Weather*, 2nd ed. (Oxford Univ. Press, 2009).

Fry, J.L., and others. *The Encyclopedia of Weather and Climate Change* (Univ. of Calif. Press, 2010).

Rupp, Rebecca. *Weather!* (Storey Kids, 2003).

Smith, Mike. *Warnings: The True Story of How Science Tamed the Weather* (Greenleaf, 2010).

Understanding the Weather (World Almanac Library, 2002).

Watts, Alan. *Instant Weather Forecasting*, 2nd ed. (Adlard Coles Nautical, 2004).

Wills, Susan, and Wills, Steven. *Meteorology: Predicting the Weather* (Oliver Press, 2004).

Yeager, Paul. *Weather Whys: Facts, Myths, and Oddities* (Penguin, 2010).